The rules of this book are few and simple: complete the most difficult challenges to get as many points as possible and become the WORLD CHAMPION.

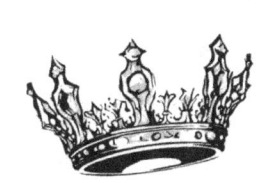
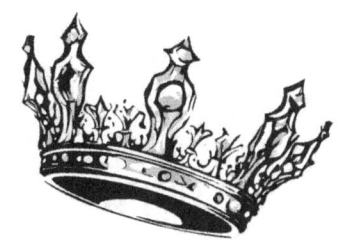

Can you handle it?

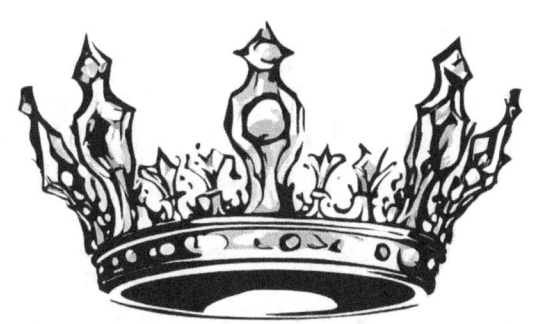

THE CHALLENGES:

-One line: 5 pts
-Black and white: 4 pts
-Never erase: 3 pts
-Less than 15 minutes: 2 pts
-Drawing completed: 1 pt

GOOD LUCK

He's going on a date

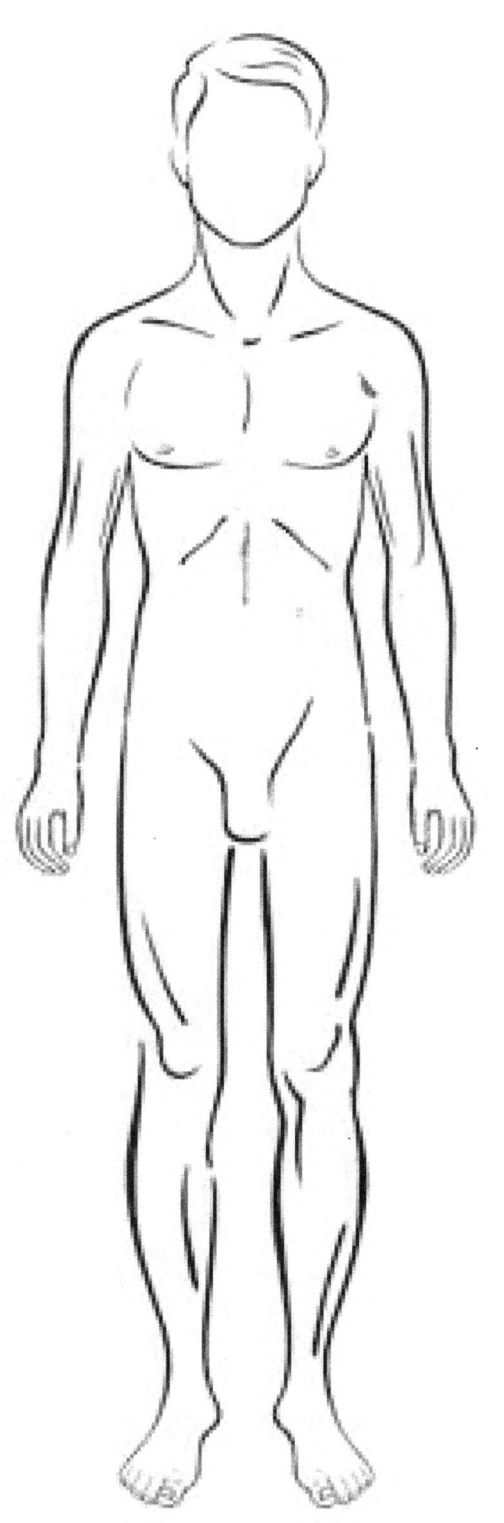

/5

He's the hero of the city

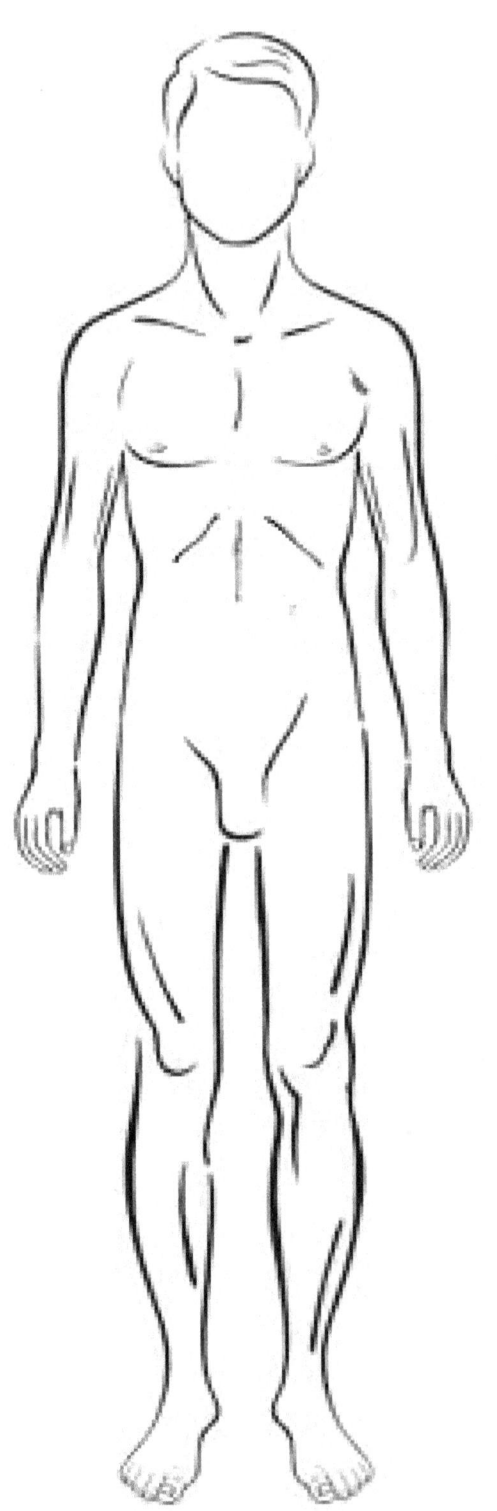

/5

He spends too much time in his room

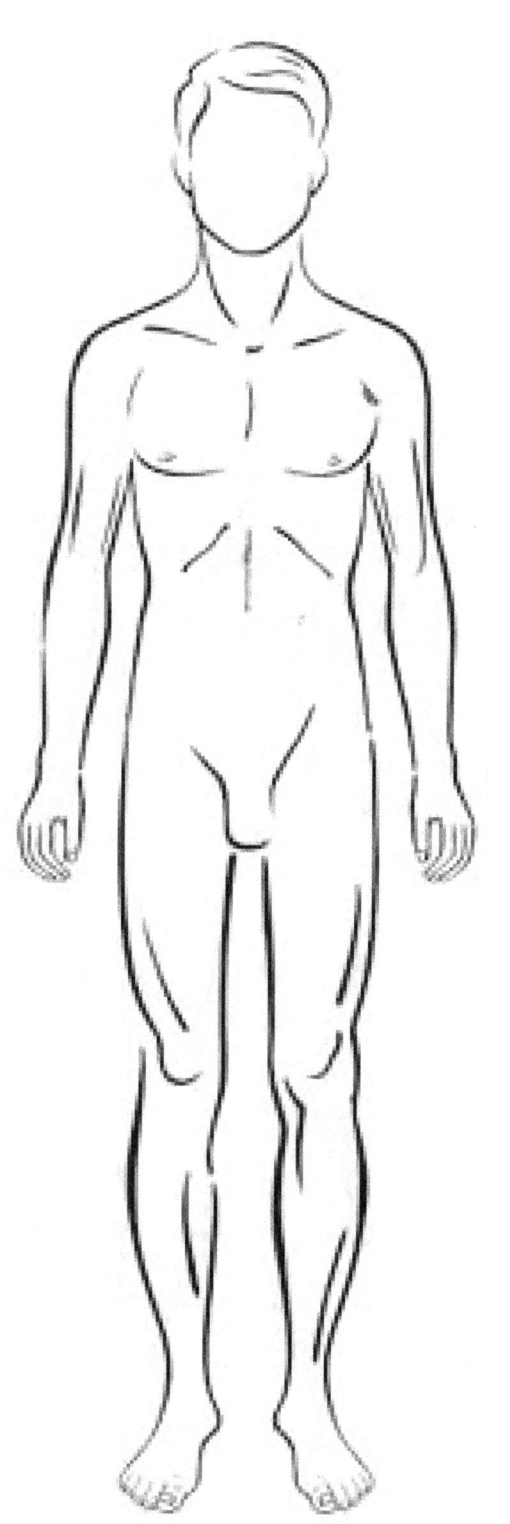

/5

He recently became rich

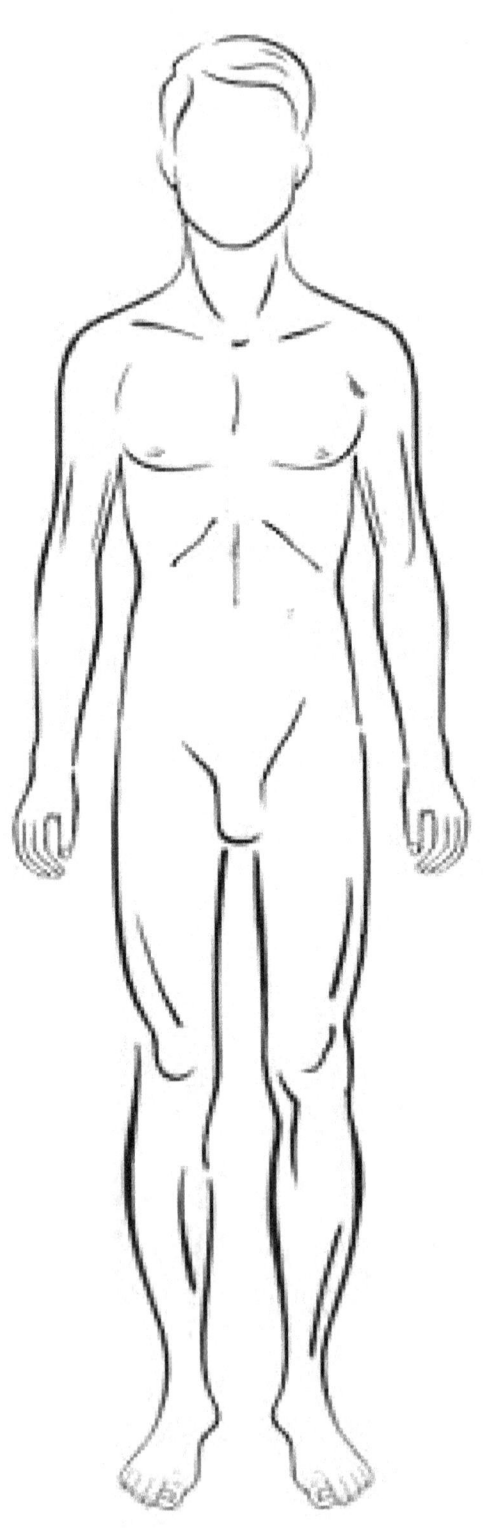

/5

He loves the pirates world

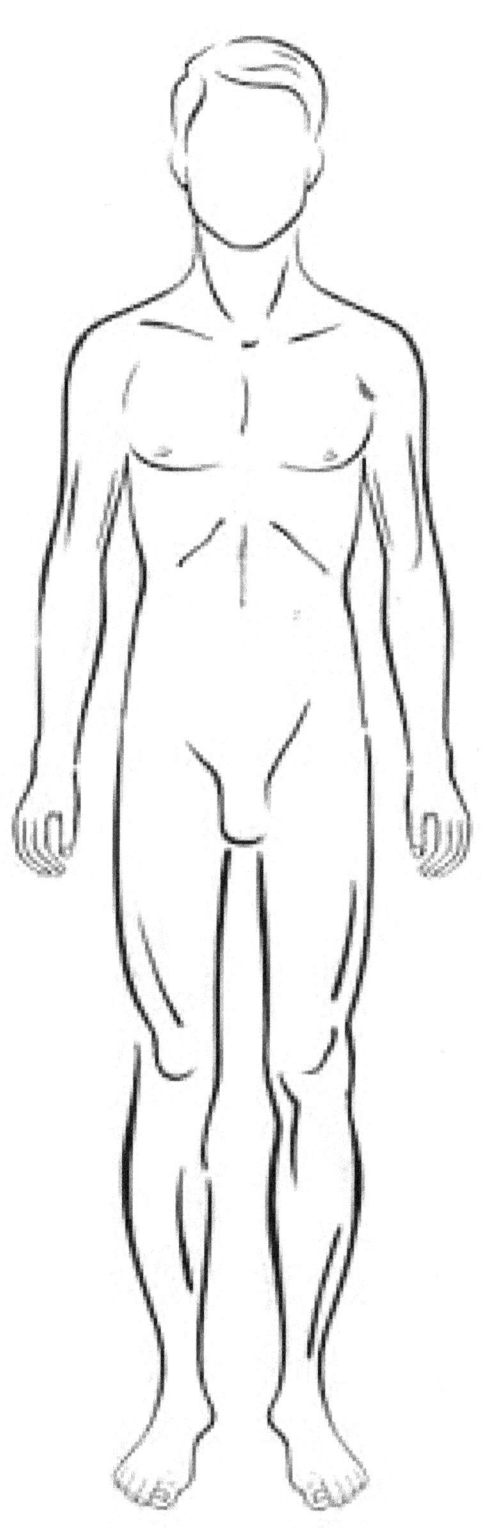

/5

He struggles to survive

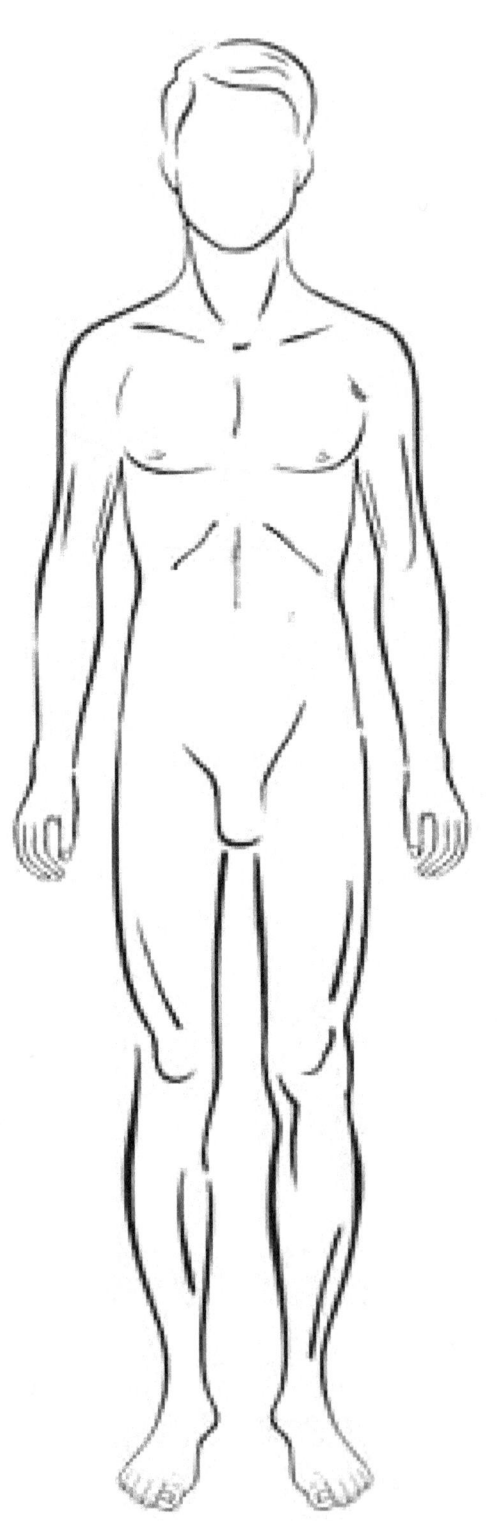

He's REALLY eccentric

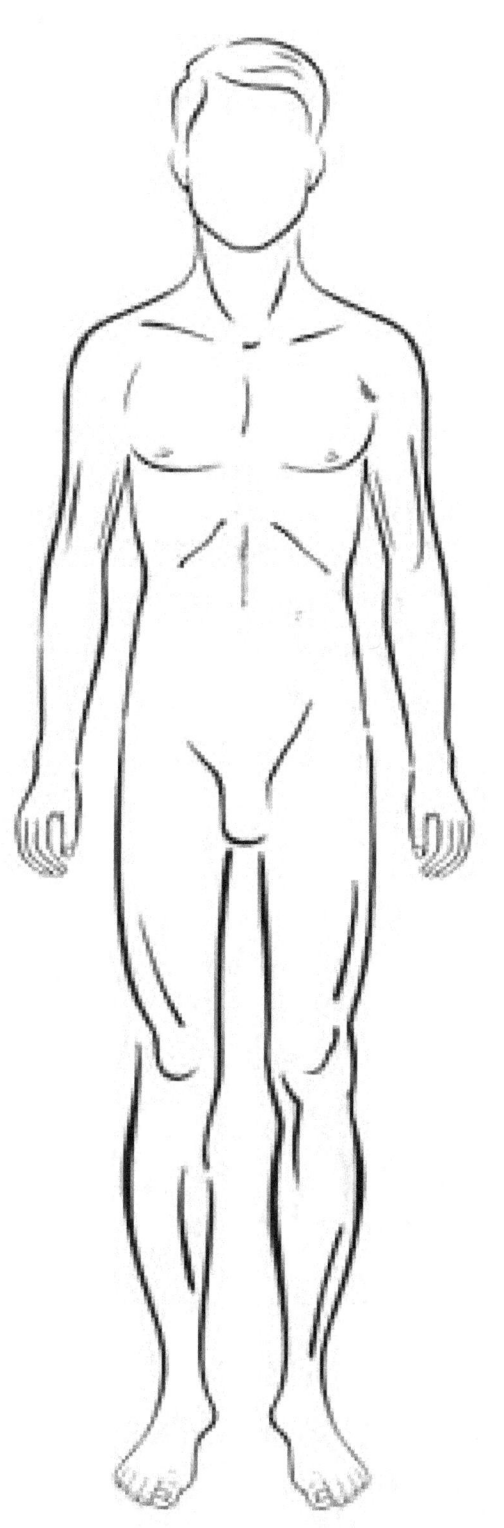

/5

He woke up with the wrong foot

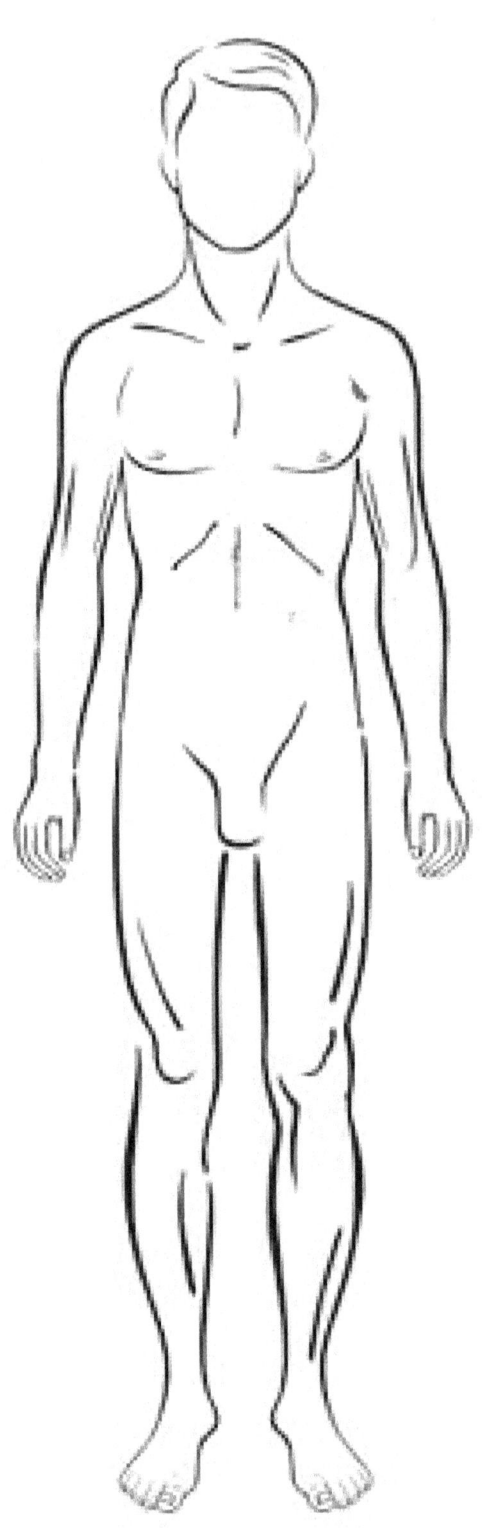

He's learning how to cook

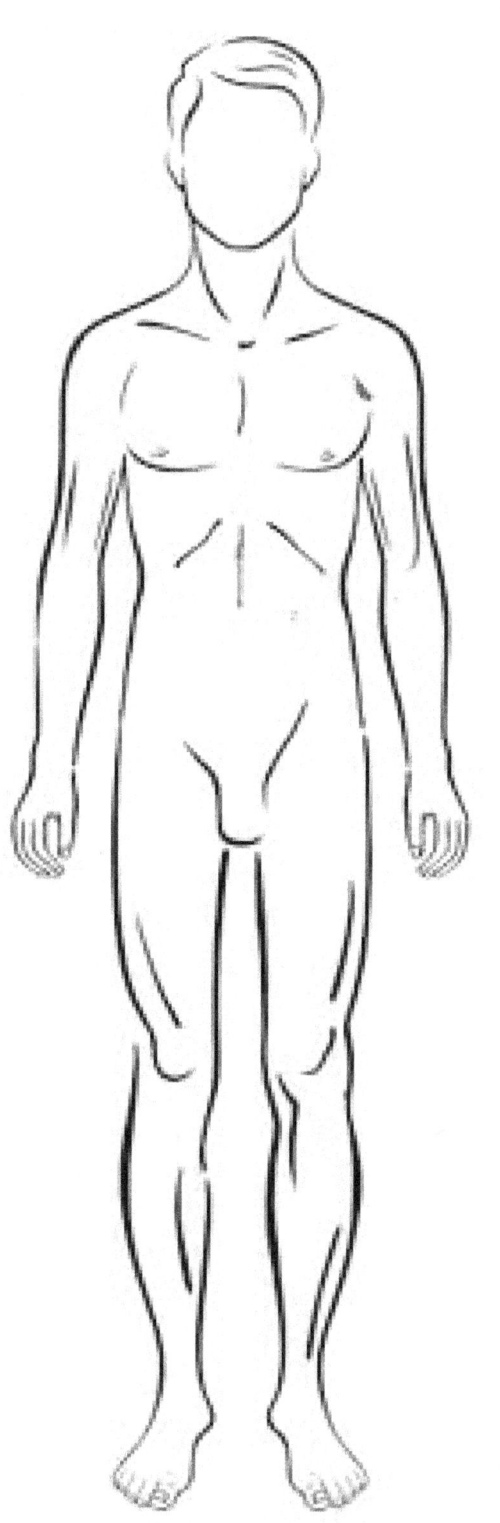

/5

He's going to an halloween party

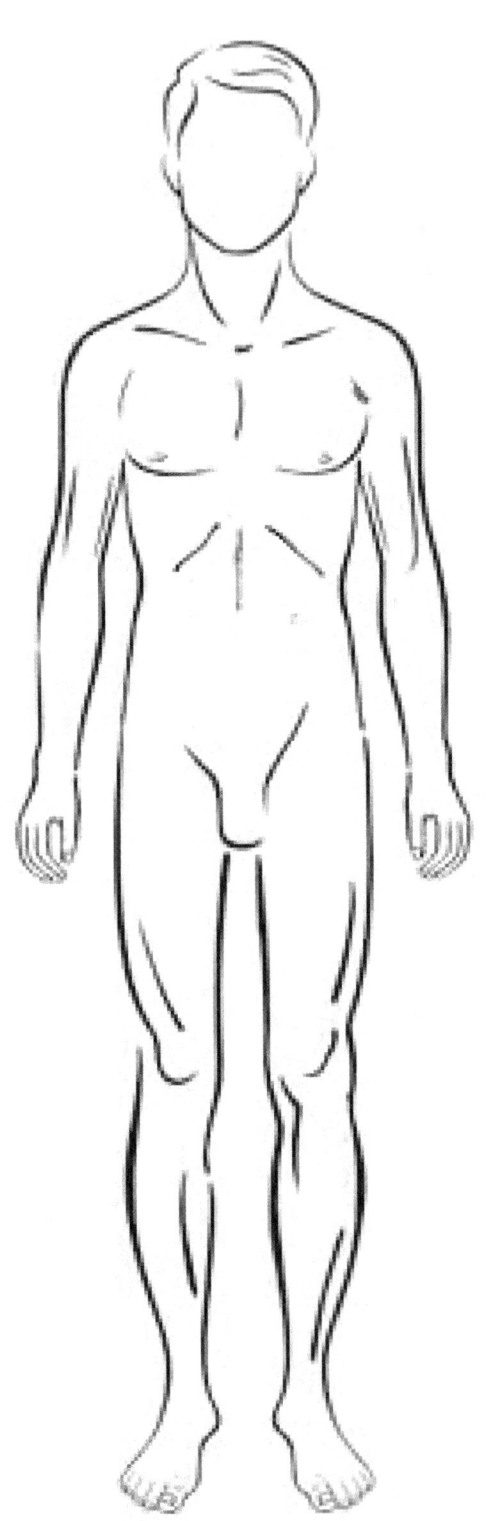

He really is into role-play

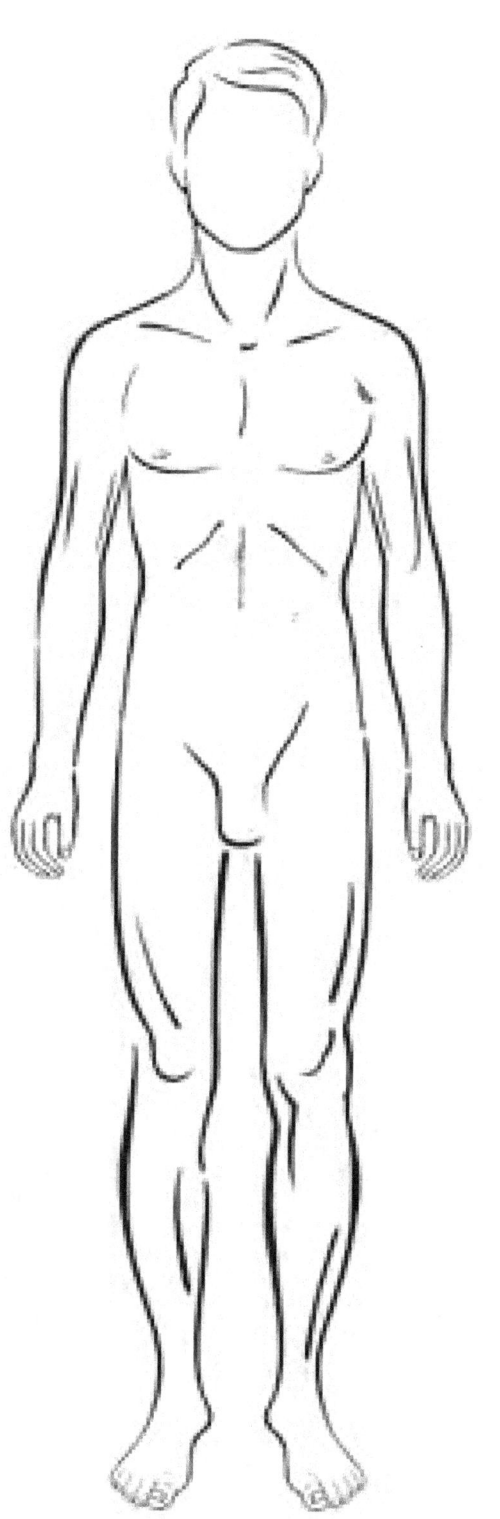

/5

He's 50 but tries to look 20

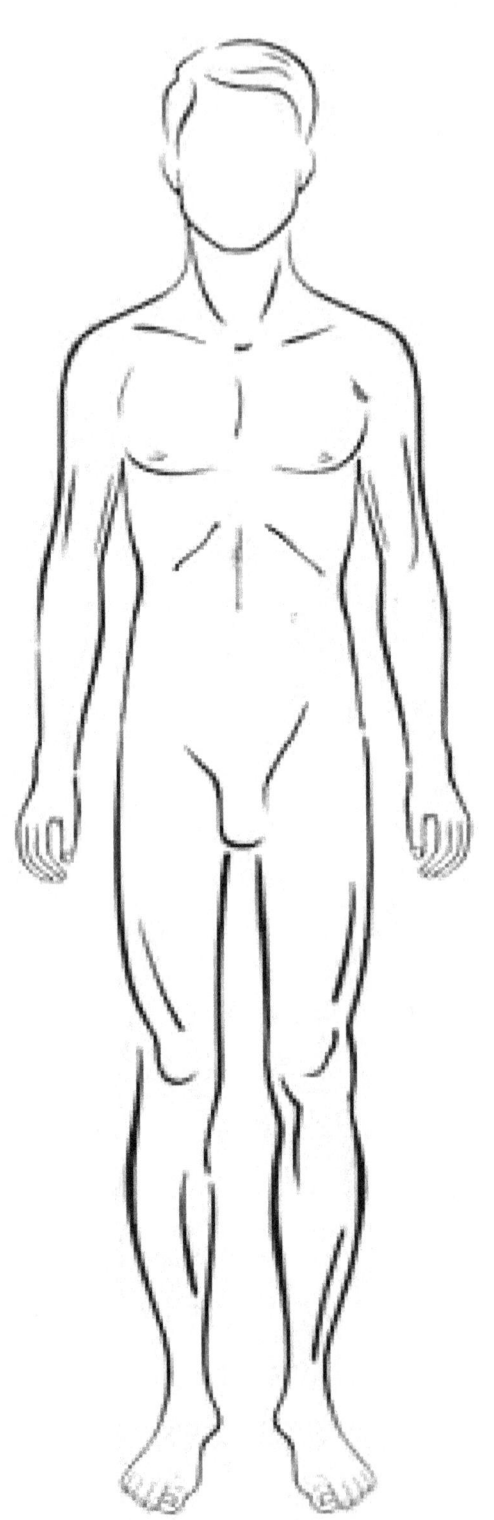

/5

He hates fast fashion

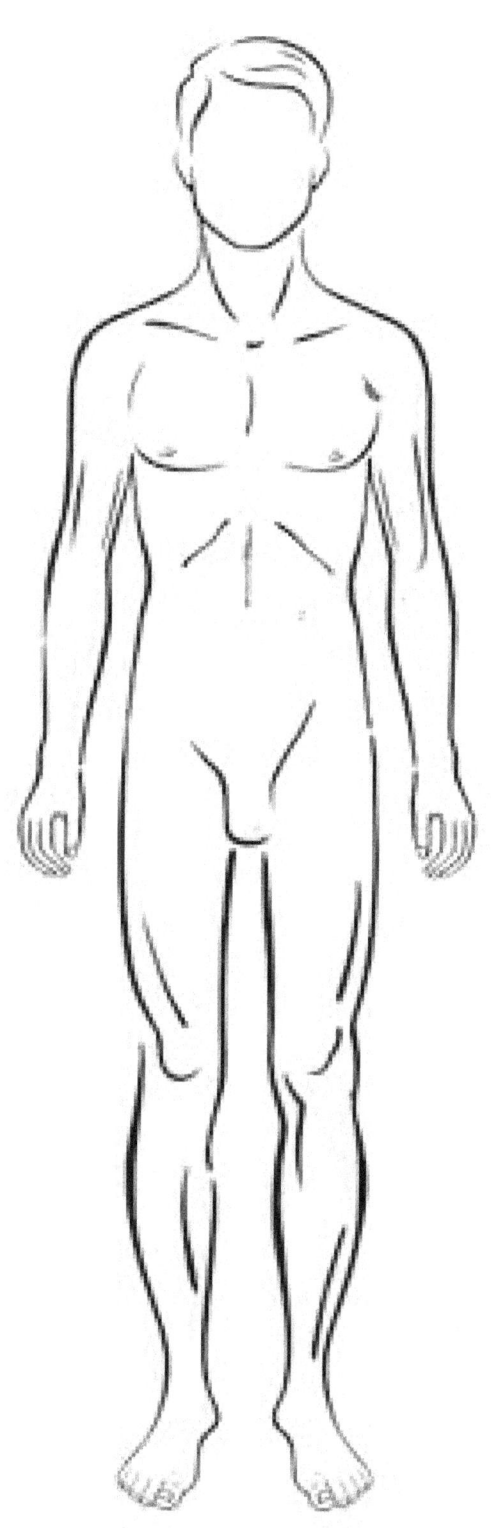

He's confident about himself

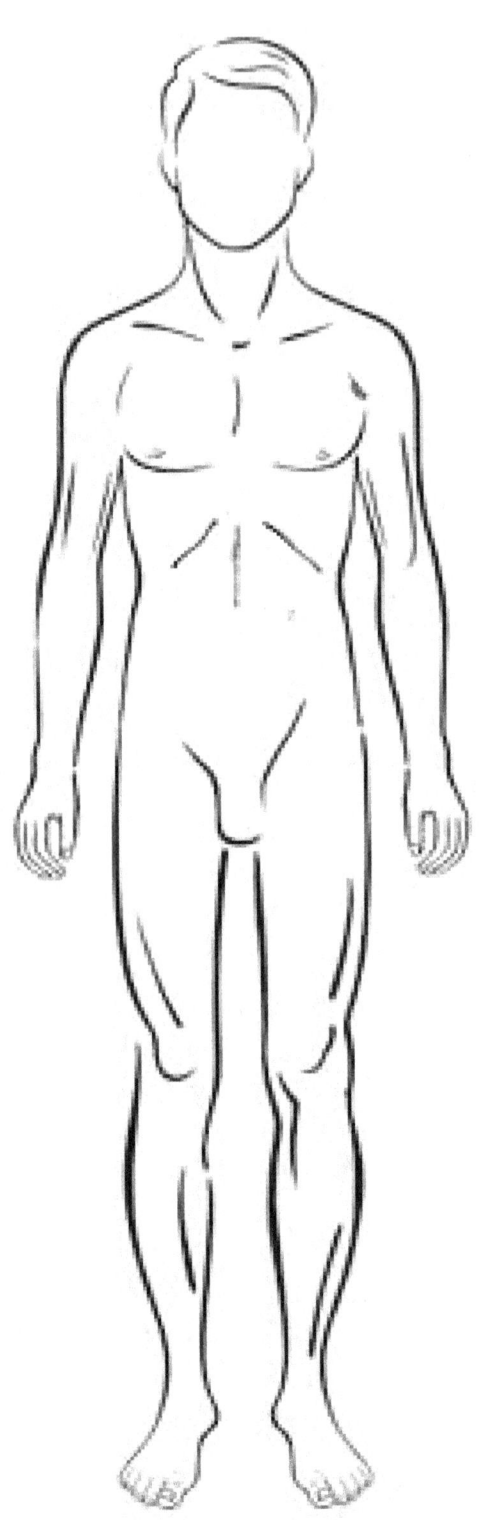

/5

He's the worst robber ever

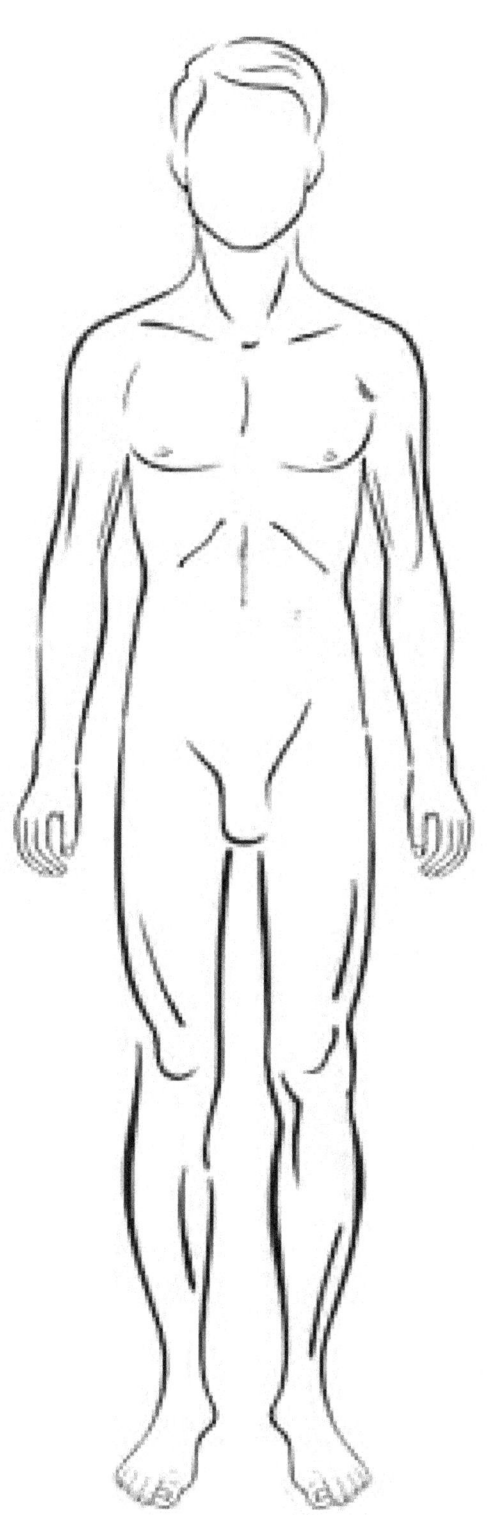

/5

He's going to Hawaii

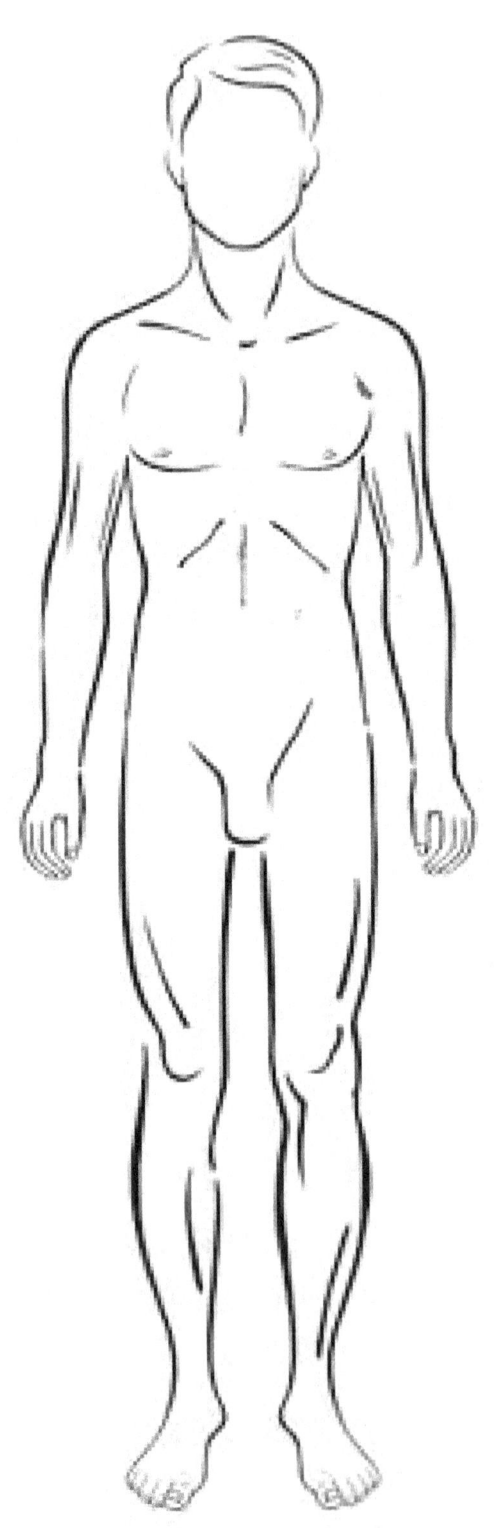

/5

He's the toughest rapper in the city

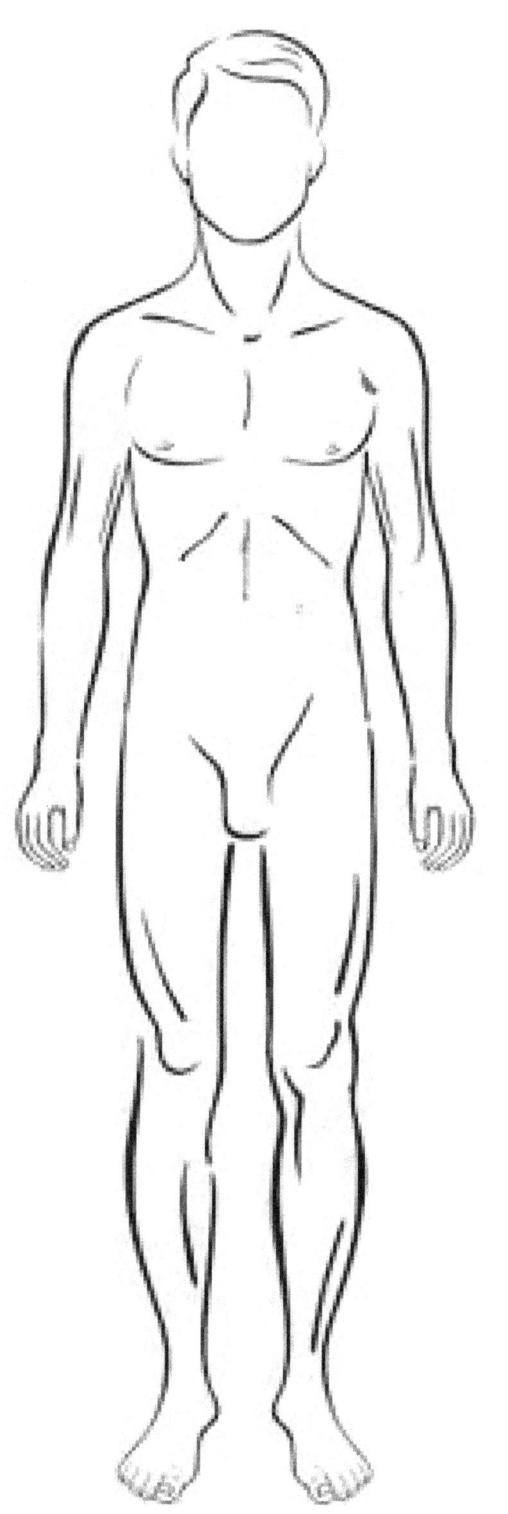

/5

He's about to get married but he's nonconformist

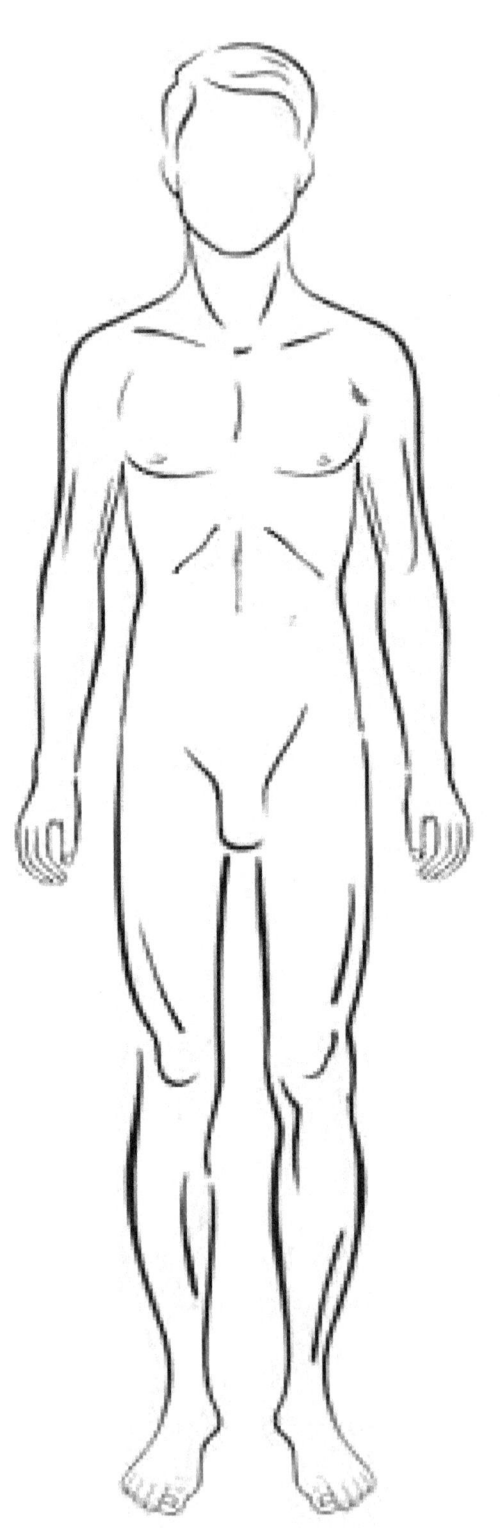

/5

He loves japanese culture

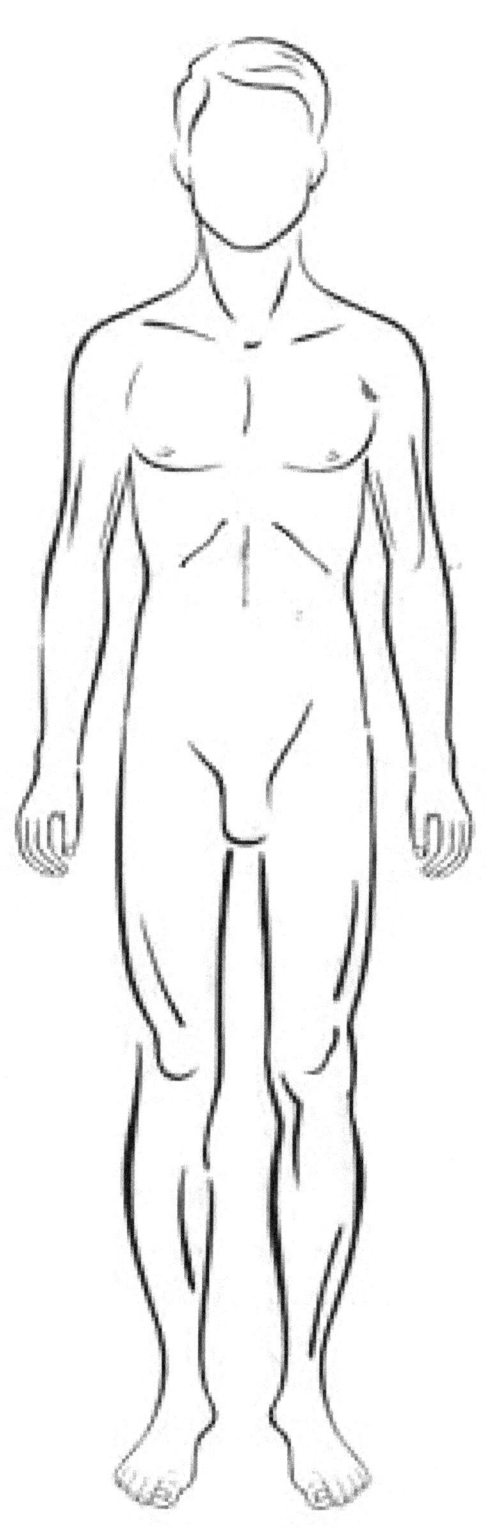

/5

He doesn't have his own style

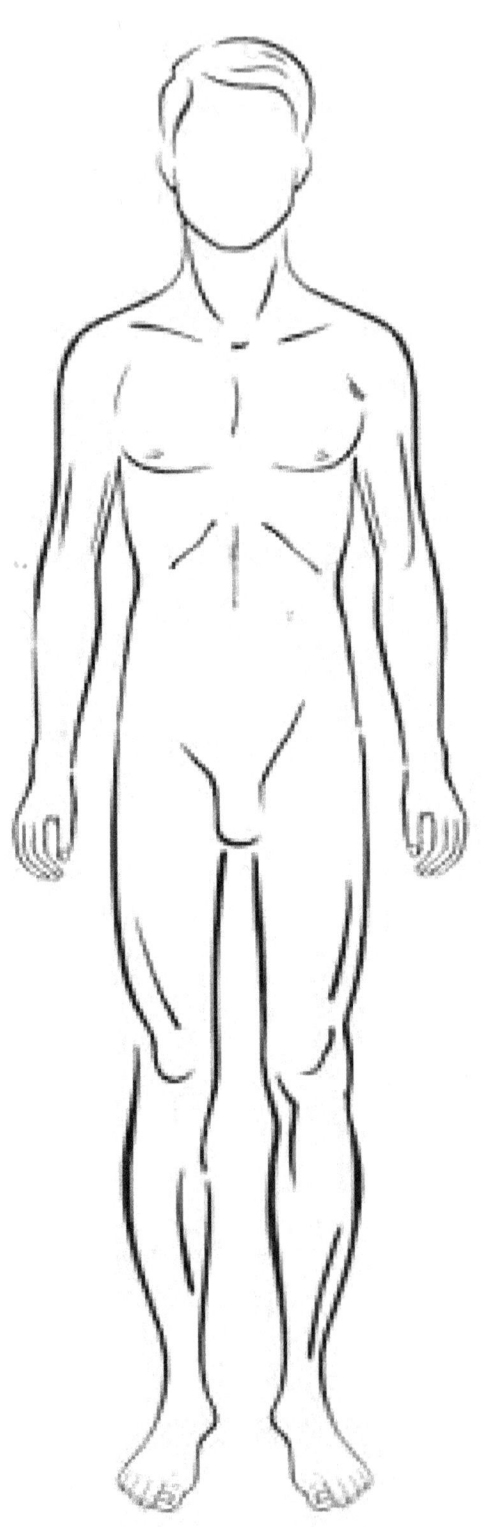

/5

He's the one that everyone hates

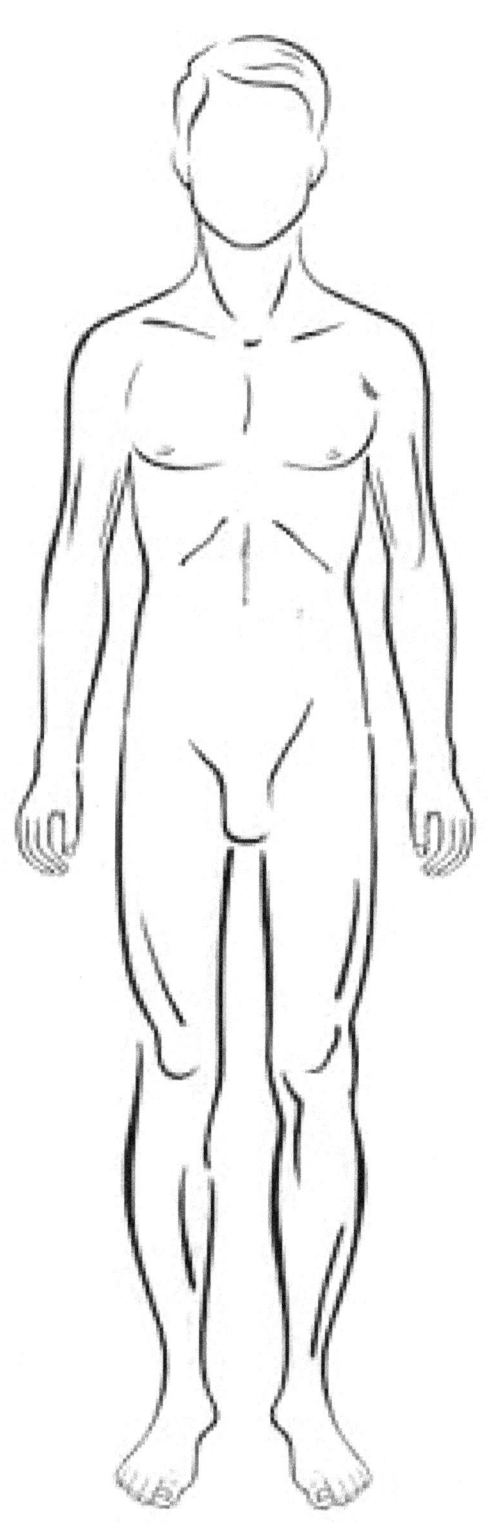

/5

He's stuck in the 90's

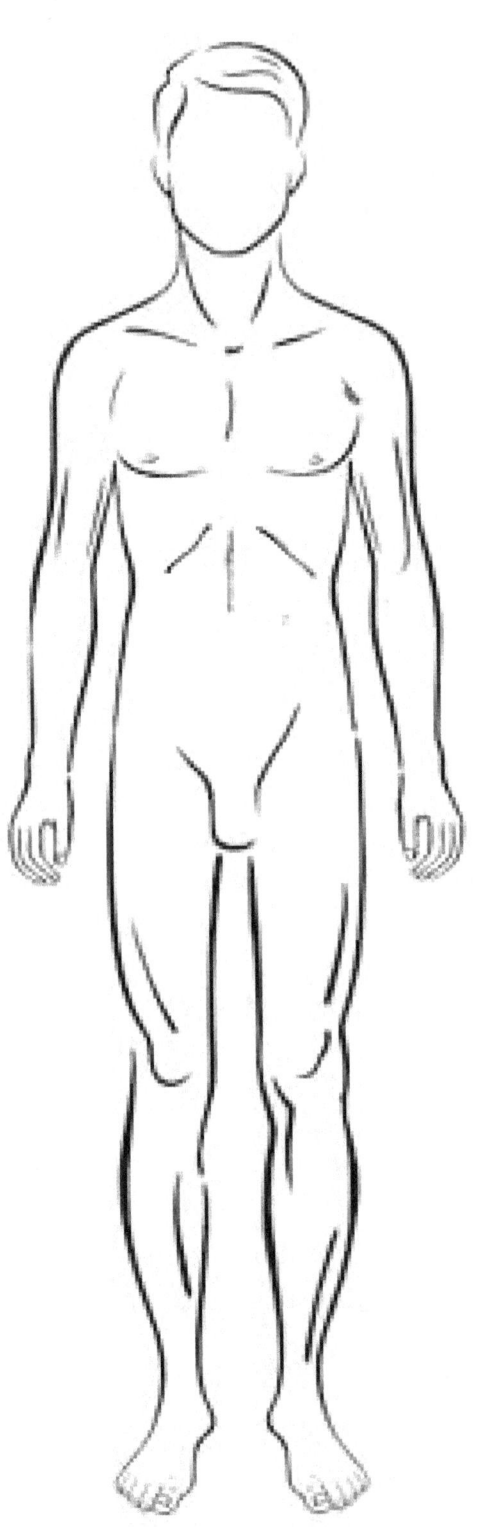

He's about to watch GOT's last episode

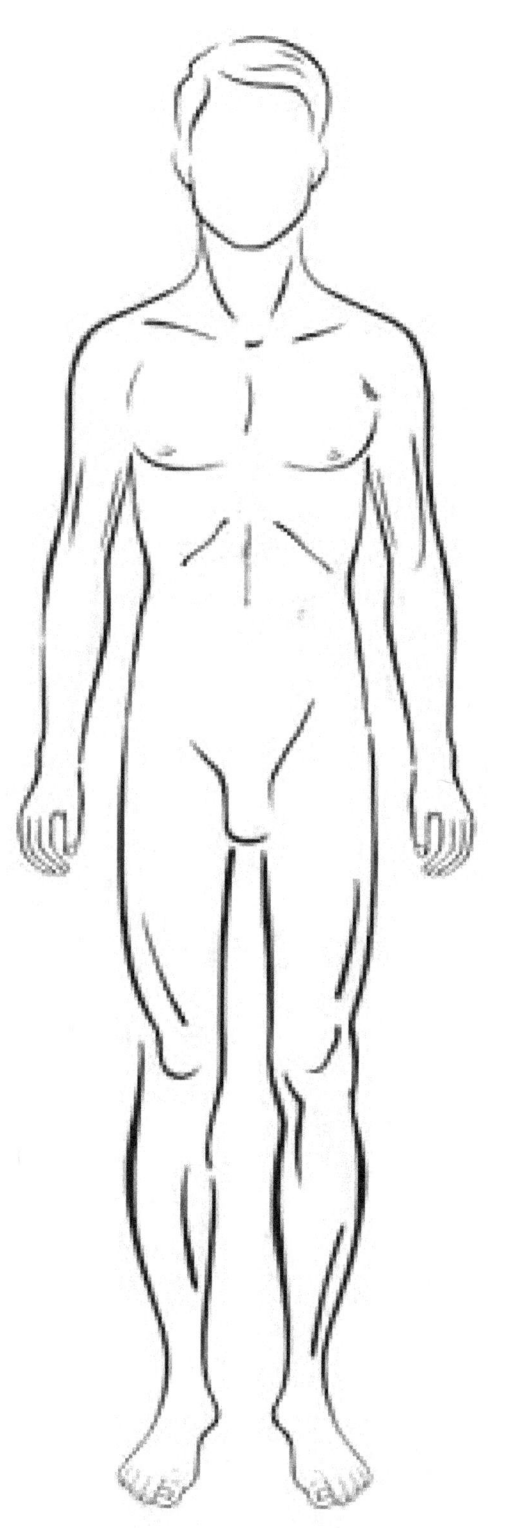

/5

He has spent 20 years living in Morocco

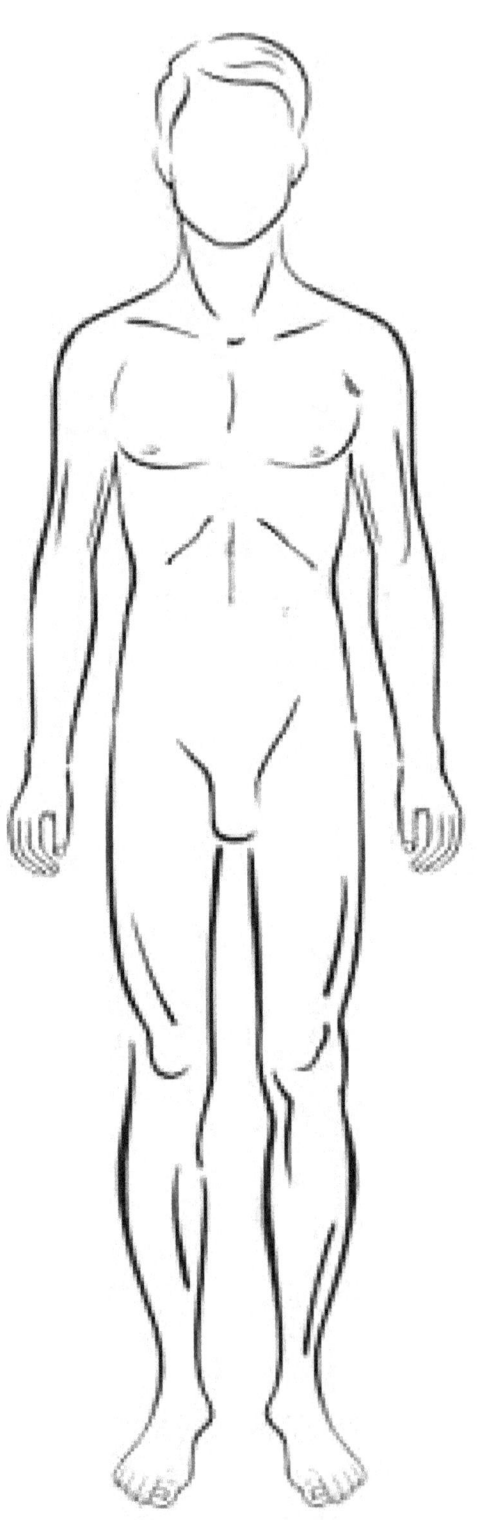

/5

He works with wild animals

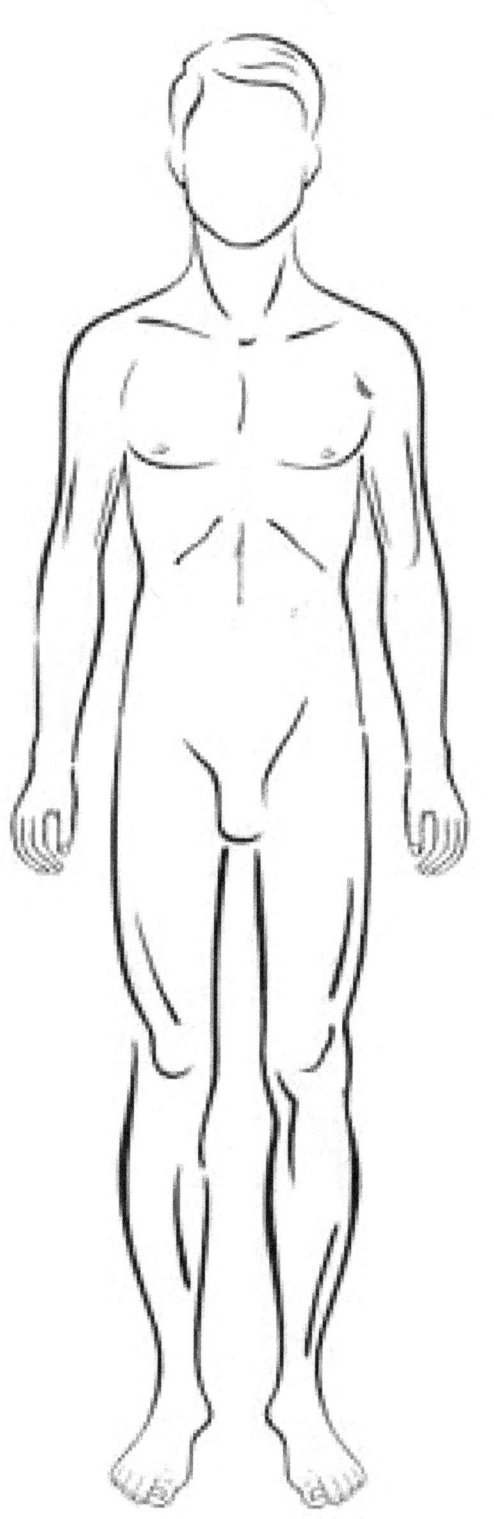

/5

He's undercover

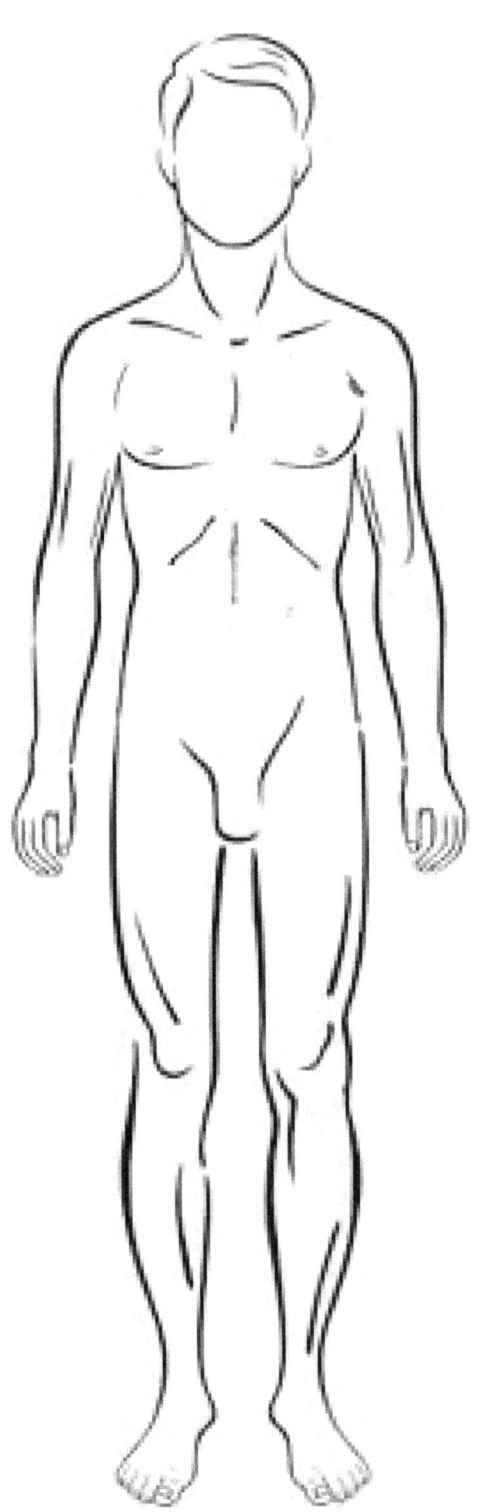

/5

He never really grew up

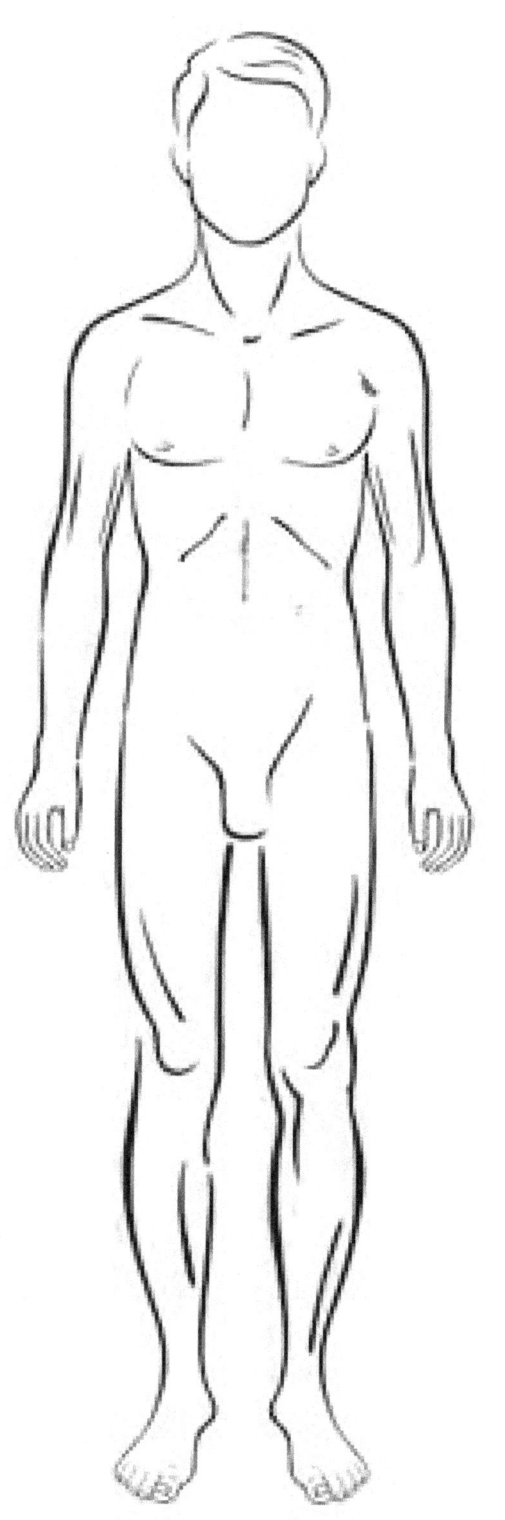

He's trying his father's old clothes

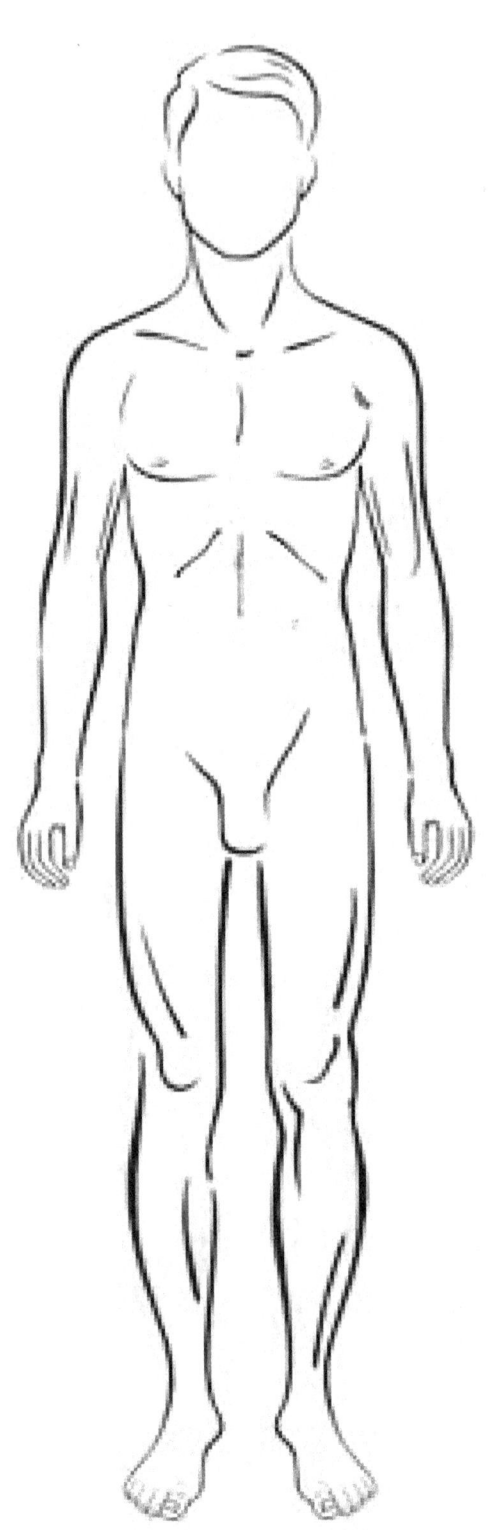

/5

He's going to protest in the square

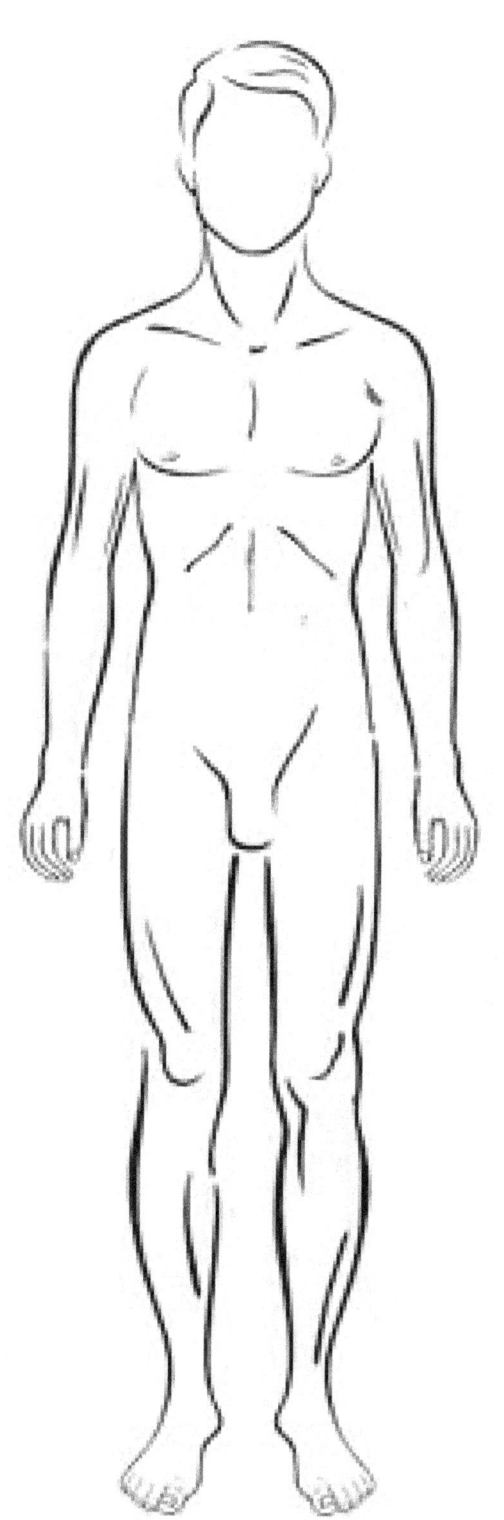

/5

He is the Prince Charming

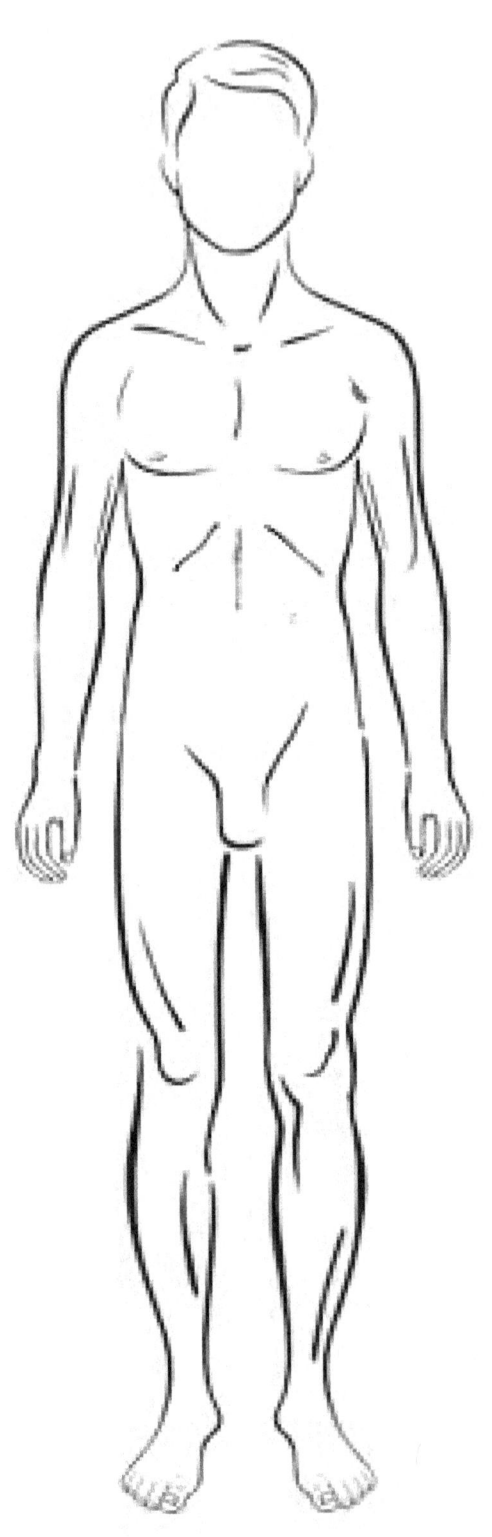

He hasn't been home in 72 hours

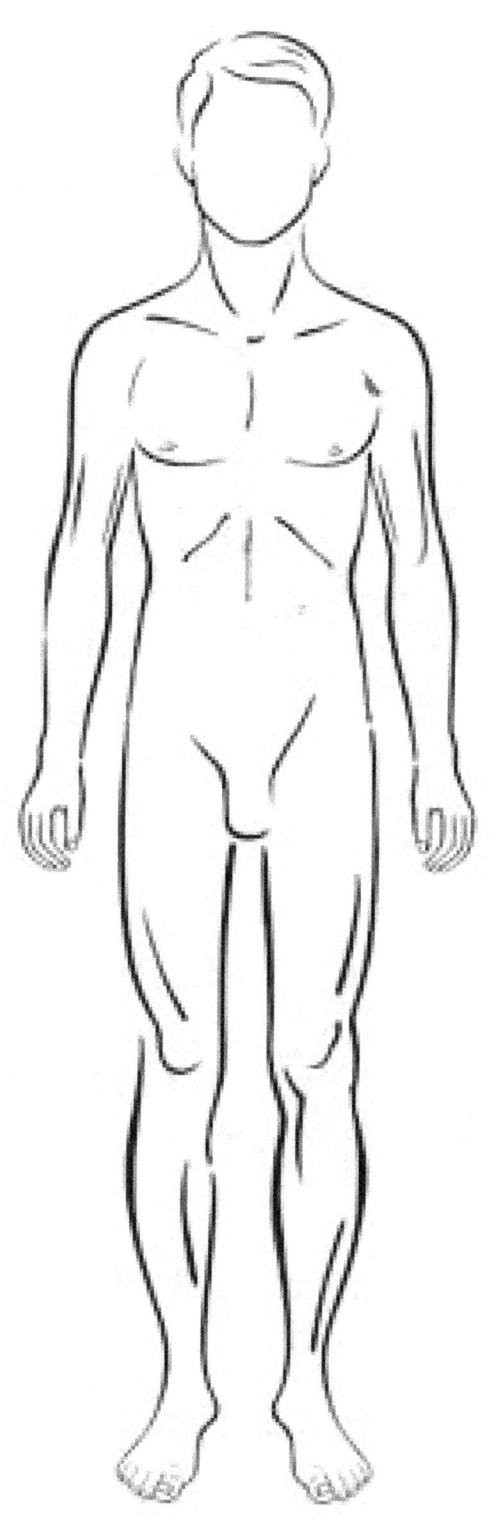

/5

Final Results:

/155

CONGRATULATIONS!

www.ingramcontent.com/pod-product-compliance
Lightning Source LLC
Chambersburg PA
CBHW081021240526
45471CB00018B/3928